DAVID KINDERSLEY
1915 – 1995

Mr Eric Gill
Letters to an
APPRENTICE

CARDOZO KINDERSLEY
2 October 1995

David with Eric Gill in the background

MR ERIC GILL

Further Thoughts by
an Apprentice

Mr Gill's ideas were of a kind that turned the prevailing hypnotic acceptance of Western art completely upside down. "He thought and then he made his thought in stone." He put the intellect at least as high as the emotions. The artist was not a special kind of man but man was a special kind of artist. Anonymity was an ideal and insofar as a work expressed the personality of the maker rather than the subject, it had failed. Such things were either accident or a hindrance to a perfect rendering of an already complete visual concept within the mind.

Mr Gill's work was deliberate and intentional – he stood apart from it being simply the executant. He was a balanced man bringing to his work an exceptional intellect, sensitivity and skill. It was in stone that these three were best united.

David Kindersley 1967

Self-portrait of David whilst at Horsham Art School

Pigotts, High Wycombe

Naphill 42
8th September 1936

Dear David,

I am very anxious to know how you are getting on and where you are. I hope you are well and working. Do write and tell us the news.

We are now at work on the Geneva panels,[1] but have not got very far yet. I wish you could come and look us up soon and then we can exchange news.

Yours, Eric Gill

Pigotts, High Wycombe

Naphill 42
19th September 1936

Dear David,

We are all very anxious to have news of you and to know your address. How are you getting on? This place is not the same since you left; we miss you very much. Many exciting things are happening – not here specially but in a general way. I have had the good fortune to receive two inspirations since I saw you last, which I will divulge when I see you. Do let us know soon where you are and how you are.

Yours, Eric Gill

Pigotts, High Wycombe

Naphill 42
2nd November 1936

Dear David,

This is just to tell you that the Exhibition at the French Gallery[2] opens on Thursday. There are three of your inscriptions in it, and I hope you will be able to look in.

Yours affectionately, Eric G

Pigotts, High Wycombe

Naphill 42
22nd January 1937

Dear David,

I was very glad to have your letter of the 19th. Please don't worry about not having replied to mine sooner. I understand fairly well the difficulties you imply, and anyway letters are always a difficult business. But I am glad to know you are alright and have got work to do. I am glad Hitchcock[3] is sending you things. I hope you are well. I am really much better and am back at work now.

I heard a rumour that the floods in the Arun Valley included your place. I hope this was not so, but I know they are very bad in the Winter as a rule.

Love from us all & someday we'll meet again.

Yours, Eric Gill

Pigotts, High Wycombe

Naphill 42
6th August 1937

Dear David,

I hear from S. and M.[4] that you are not doing anything for them at present and therefore might be free to do a job for me. Is that so? If it is I will write again sending sketch, etc. The job is a large gravestone to be fixed in Chichester Cemetery.[5] It consists of a slab lying on the grave, supported on a plinth. On the top face will be a long inscription in 1¾" letters with a crest in incised lines at the head (the crest is some kind of bird standing on a crown holding a cross in its mouth), and round the edges of the stone two lines of smaller letters – about 600 letters in all. The top stone will be about 6'6" x 3'0" x 6" and the plinth stones will be about 6" thick, so that the whole thing stands 9" or 10" above ground. I do hope you can do this job as it is wanted by September 5th (date of "unveiling").

I hear of you from time to time: I hope you are getting on alright and wish we could see you. Everybody is well here and the Geneva job is going strong at present, also several tombstones. We've been doing some in slate lately, which is beautiful for lettering.

Yours affectionately, Eric Gill

SACRED TO THE MEMORY OF
JOHN WILLIAM MADDEN ×
CAPTAIN, ADJUTANT OF THE RYL.
SUSSEX LIGHT INFANTRY, BORN
1828, DIED AT CHICHESTER, 1875
AND OF HIS SON
CHARLES EDWARD MADDEN ×
ADMIRAL OF THE FLEET, FIRST
BARONET OF KELLS, Co. KILKENNY
G.C.B., O.M., G.C.V.O., K.C.M.G., D.C.L. OXON., LL.D.
BORN 5TH. SEPTEMBER, 1862
CHIEF OF STAFF AND SECOND IN
COMMAND, GRAND FLEET, 1914-19
COMMANDER-IN-CHIEF ATLANTIC
FLEET, 1919-22, FIRST SEA LORD
1927-30, DIED 5TH. JUNE, 1935

THIS STONE REPLACES THE CROSS
ERECTED TO THE MEMORY OF
CAPTAIN MADDEN BY THE OFFICERS
& NON-COMMISSIONED OFFICERS
OF HIS REGIMENT & WAS PLACED
HERE BY CONSTANCE WINIFRED
WIFE OF CHARLES EDWARD MADDEN
IN LOVING MEMORY OF HIS NOBLE
LIFE AND IN REMEMBRANCE OF
HIS DEVOTION TO HER AND
TO THEIR CHILDREN

2"

2"

N.B. this line marks the end of the flat top surface. There will be no actual line on the stone.

Section

top slab 5"

plinth 7"

3"

2½"

N.B. all letters 1¾"
except the two marked ×
all spaces 1"
except top & bottom

1' 2¼"
Space for crest

1¼" to be formed.

1½"

n Madden

AL

PS

1 day to shift stone
2 days to finish drawing
8 days to cut
3 days for [illegible] 1

14

Pigotts, High Wycombe

Naphill 42
10th August 1937

Dear David,

I was very glad to hear from you. S. & M. are sending you a copy of the drawing which I have sent them.[6] I hope they will be able to arrange with Messrs. Taylor[7] to do the masonry and to deliver the top slab to you at Horsham. I will let you have a detail of the crest in good time. I don't think you will require a drawing of the lettering. The perspective sketch shows exactly how it is to be arranged. I think you will find that it is possible to do the lettering on the top in 1¾" letters, with 1" spaces, and the lettering round the sides in 1½". I am relying on you to carry the work out in the tradition of this shop, i.e. plain Roman letters, and as the job is for the open air the letters should be deeply cut and not too much thick and thin.

Yours, Eric G

SACRED TO THE MEMORY OF
JOHN WILLIAM MADDEN
CAPTAIN & ADJUTANT OF THE
ROYAL SUSSEX LIGHT INFANTRY
BORN [illegible]
DIED AT CHICHESTER, 1875
AND OF HIS SON
CHARLES EDWARD MADDEN
ADMIRAL OF THE FLEET
FIRST BARONET OF KELLS
CO. KILKENNY
G.C.B., O.M., G.C.V.O., K.C.M.G
D.C.L. OXON, LL.D.
BORN 5TH. SEPTEMBER, 1862
CHIEF OF STAFF AND
SECOND IN COMMAND
GRAND FLEET, 1914-1919
COMMANDER-IN-CHIEF
ATLANTIC FLEET, 1919-1922
FIRST SEA LORD, 1927-1930
DIED 5TH. JUNE, 1935

THIS STONE REPLACES THE CROSS ERECTED TO THE MEMORY OF CAPTAIN
MADDEN BY THE OFFICERS & NON COMMISSIONED OFFICERS OF HIS REGIMENT
AND WAS PLACED HERE
BY CONSTANCE WINIFRED

(i.e. 6' 0" flat surface only see f.s. d.)

Joint

Joint

5" 7"

Madden

Portland Stone
— 6' 6" long by 3' 0" wide
by 12" high (including plinth)
(for Chichester Cemetery)

EG 5.8.37

Pigotts, High Wycombe

Naphill 42
11th August 1937

Dear David,

Many thanks for yours of yesterday. Herewith I enclose the detail of crest[8] as mentioned in the letter written yesterday, which I send also. I hope I shall be able to see you next week. I am not sure yet what day it will be, but probably Wednesday.

Yours, Eric G

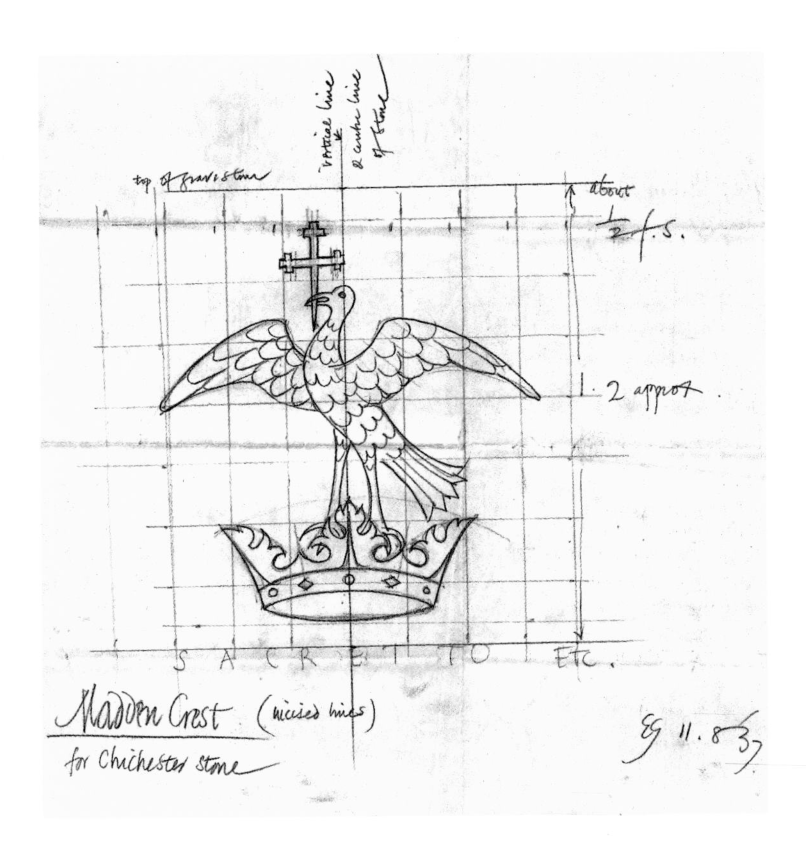

n Madden inscript (Chichester)

25 lines of letters @ $1\frac{3}{4}$" = ~~43~~ $43\frac{3}{4}$"

2 " " 2" 4"

$47\frac{3}{4}$"

Total space for lettering 7'.6" = 90"

space left for Crest & spaces $42\frac{1}{4}$"

Crest 1. $2\frac{1}{4}$ $14\frac{1}{4}$

28"

~~25~~ 1" spaces between lines 25"

Top & bottom spaces $1\frac{1}{2}$ = 3"

28"

Q.E.F.

E.G. 27.8.37

PIGOTTS / HIGH WYCOMBE / TEL: NAPHILL 42

30. 11. '37

Dear David: Many thanks for yours of 29th.
I'm sorry about the difficulty of the Madden cost, but I'm glad you think Lady M. will now be satisfied. If I get ½ a chance I'll go & have a look at the stone in Chichester cemetery. I'm sure what you've done with the sizes of letters is quite all right. I'm jolly keen to see what sort of a job you make of lettering on your own! I wish you'd send me a rubbing sometimes. I wish you were here with us now. Yes, I badly want a mason — because the Geneva job is taking all hands & the tombstones etc. are in arrears.

Oh yes — I know about Sir Arnold W. & his Franco biz. It's difficult, because one can't be said to know the truth. If you were asked to inscribe something you knew to be false & bad then you could justly prefer to starve. But, as in this Spanish biz., when the whole thing is doubtful — both sides right, both wrong — then, I judge, you shd. regard it simply as a job of lettercutting and do it as you do the fatuous compositions of some of our widows. I'm v. sorry about it. An enormous proportion of work to-day is in same category. On other hand if you were luckily so full up with work as not to need the Alcazar job, then that is just the kind of job to turn down. Lor! what a difficult life. Be wise as serpents & harmless as doves! Look before you leap, but remember: he that hesitates is lost...

Love from all here Yours Eric G

So: if you've enough work otherwise, turn Sir A. W. down.,
otherwise regard it as a job of lettercutting — unless you know it's bad lies.

Pigotts, High Wycombe Naphill 42
30. 11. '37

Dear David: Many thanks for yours of 29th. I'm sorry about the difficulty of the Madden crest, but I'm glad you think Lady M. will now be satisfied. If I get ½ a chance I'll go & have a look at the stone in Chichester cemetery. I'm sure what you've done with the sizes of letters is quite all right. I'm jolly keen to see what sort of a job you make of lettering on your own! I wish you'd send me a rubbing sometimes. I wish you were here with us now. Yes, I badly want a mason – because the Geneva job is taking all hands & the tombstones etc. are in arrears.

Oh yes – I know about Sir Arnold W. & his Franco biz.[9] It's difficult, because one can't be said to know the truth. If you were asked to inscript. something you *knew* to be false & bad then you could justly prefer to starve. But, as in this Spanish biz., when the whole thing is doubtful – both sides right, both wrong – then, I judge, you shd. regard it simply as a job of lettercutting and do it as you do the fatuous compositions of some of our widows. I'm v. sorry about it. An enormous proportion of work today is in same category. On other hand if you were luckily so full up with work as not to need the Alcazar job, then that is just the kind of job to turn down. Lor! what a difficult life. Be wise as serpents & harmless as doves! Look before you leap, but remember: he that hesitates is lost ....

Love from all here. Yours, Eric G

So : if you've enough work otherwise, turn Sir A.W. down. Otherwise regard it as a job of lettercutting – unless you know it's bad lies.

Pigotts, High Wycombe

Naphill 42
15th September 1938

David Kindersley Esq.,
56 Park Street,
Horsham, Sussex.

Dear David,

I am pleased to hear from you again and to know that you are fairly busy. I am glad you are in touch with S. & M.

I will speak to Denis[10] about the brass tablet[11] and ask him to write to you, but if he cannot do it the best man to go to is Mr George Friend of 321 High Holborn. He has done lots of these for me, but it would be nice if you could get Denis to do it.

Yes, the Geneva work is now actually finished. I got back from Geneva about a fortnight ago. Anthony[12] went with me and we spent a week there touching it up and polishing. It does not look too bad, but the world verdict has not yet been published – waiting, I expect, for Musso and Hitler to have a look and decide what they think.

Do come and see us if you get half a chance. I am always wondering how you are and what you are doing.

Yours sincerely,
Eric Gill
pp HNT

Pigotts, High Wycombe

Naphill 42
16th February 1939

David Kindersley Esq.,
The Old Bakehouse,
The Haven, Billingshurst.

Dear David,

I was very sorry indeed not to see you before you left and I am also very sorry not to have seen more of you while you were here.[13] Life is rather hectic for me at present and I do not seem to have any chance of a quiet conversation with anybody. I meant to have given you the enclosed, so now send it.[14]

I will let you know if it seems necessary to get you down for a day next week. Thank you very much indeed for what you have done and let me have your bill. I hope we shall meet again before long.

Yours affectionately, Eric G

Pigotts, High Wycombe

Naphill 42
20th February 1939

David Kindersley Esq.,
The Old Bakehouse,
The Haven,
Billingshurst, Sussex.

Dear David,

Many thanks for yours.[15] Herewith cheque and I will let you know how the stones fit when fixed.

Yours, Eric G

Eric Gill at Guildford Cathedral

Guildford Dec. 19 '39

My dear David – what a bore & more than a bore – I've finished the job here this very day & go home to-morrow![16] I wish, I wish I had communicated before. I hoped that my host here wd. have been able to bring me over to see you but lack of Petrol has kept his car in garage. Yes, I heard of your marriage – Anthony had talk with Mr Shadwick in hospital.[17] He asked Anthony, straight out of the blue, so to say, if he knew you! & A. said "I do indeed; do you?" I was very glad to hear of your marriage. I'm always glad to hear of marriages & especially of those I love. What fun! What joy! and God bless it & you & her. So I am dreadfully sorry my time here has come to an end for the present. I've got another carving to do here but it won't be till about next August, because the wall isn't up yet as high as the place where it's to go.[18]

How are you & are you busy? I've got tons to do. I shall miss Anthony very much. He is to be married on Jan 2, I think, and is going to live & farm at a place called Laxton near Kettering in Northants. (address: A.F., *Upper* Laxton). Poor Anthony he did have a bad time & is much pulled down in consequence (looks even more too-good-to-be-true than usual)

Dear David, I'm so sorry not to be seeing you here. Wish you could get over to Pigotts & bring your wife & son with you, but I fear that's an impossibility – isn't it? I've been absolutely tied to the job here – what with the weather & short days & having to go off to do other things (lectures here & there & alternate weekends at home to keep things going there, etc.) I haven't had a moment on weekdays & on Sundays I've generally had an accumulation of letters to write. So there it is, but it does seem a shame to be so near & not see you.

Yrs. affectly, Eric Gill

Drawing in red ink from Eric Gill to David

The moment I met David, in 1975 at an ATypI conference in Poland, I knew I was to be his apprentice. It was as if a 'concept' deep within myself had all of a sudden become reality.

His abrupt first words which burnt into my mind were: "I hate things almost perfect!" I still don't know whether that referred to something he had just seen or to the impact our meeting had on him. To my wish to work with him – which he had seen even before I uttered it – he replied: "You have the vital energy and purpose that makes the thing go."

David was to me as he had described Mr. Gill: "He was a balanced man bringing to his work an exceptional intellect, sensitivity and skill." But above all he was a man of great humility, or as the Abbot of Ampleforth described him, a wise man in the spirit of Solomon.

When in Autumn 1977 we had moved into a new workshop and into a new life, he pictured our love in one of his many and so beautiful letters he wrote to me during that time: "You have moved me into the new workshop and now you will move both of us on the road of creation with tender hands and loving caresses."

Lida Lopes Cardozo 1995

David Kindersley went to work with Eric Gill in 1934 and stayed until June 1936. When David left to 'go it alone' they remained close friends. Gill continued to ask after him and he sent on the occasional commission as shown in these letters. They also reveal the respect and affection that the two men held for each other, both in Gill's expressively 'open' comments and in the light-hearted banter. One wonders what the "two inspirations" mentioned in the second letter were!

Eric Gill made a lasting impression on David Kindersley's whole attitude to life and work – nothing was the same afterwards. These letters are reproduced here as a tribute to David's life and the work he went on to achieve, thanks to "Mr Gill".

Guy Bettley-Cooke 1995

Notes

1. The three relief-carved 'Creation' panels for the Assembly Hall of the League of Nations building in Geneva, Switzerland
2. The exhibition, 'Eric Gill and Companions' was held at the French Gallery, 11 Berkeley Square, London, until 26th November 1936; the three works referred to were:

i)	In hoc cognovimus…	Hopton-Wood stone	£12.0.0
ii)	Et alias oves…	Hopton-Wood stone	£7.0.0
iii)	Shorthand Tombstone (Gregg)	Hopton-Wood stone	£5.0.0

   Apart from Gill and Kindersley, the other 'companions' showing work were Lawrence Cribb, Anthony Foster and Donald Potter
3. Eldred F. Hitchcock, business manager of 'Sculpture & Memorials Ltd' of 26 Albemarle Street, London – a firm created to promote and gain commissions for fine quality memorial craftsmen
4. 'Sculpture & Memorials Ltd', see above
5. A Portland stone ledger, in memory of Captain John William Madden (1828–1875), and his son, Admiral Charles Edward Madden (1862–1935)
6. Early copy-reproduction of perspective design for the Madden ledger, signed and dated EG 5.8.37
7. 'Taylor Bros' of 195A Warwick Road, Kensington, London. Fixer masons to 'Sculpture & Memorials Ltd'
8. 'Squared-up' design for the Madden Crest, with measurements, signed and dated E.G. 11.8.'37
9. Sir Arnold Wilson, Conservative MP and ardent Franco supporter, commissioned Kindersley to carve a tablet dedicated to 'The Heroes of The Alcazar', for eventual erection at The Alcazar itself, in Toledo, Spain. It *was* duly carved and remains there (or a good copy of it does) to this day
10. Denis Tegetmeier, husband of Petra (née Gill), engraver, illustrator, painter, and later, memorial designer
11. A memorial brass dedicated to the memory of Admiral William Wordsworth Fisher (1875–1937), and his son, Nevil (1914–1935), designed by Kindersley and engraved by G.T. Friend, as suggested by Gill; erected in Brockenhurst Church, Hampshire
12. Anthony Foster, carving assistant to Eric Gill from 1933 until 1940
13. Kindersley returned to 'Pigotts' to assist with the carving of keystones for use in the Gill-designed Church of St Peter the Apostle, Gorlestone-on-Sea, Norfolk
14. Unclear, possibly a 'reading list' of twenty-two book titles, written in Gill's hand
15. Kindersley's bill, as requested in the previous letter : 'Working Bath Stone at 1/6 an hour. 27 hours. £2.0s.6d'
16. The carvings on Guildford Cathedral, Surrey: St John the Baptist and the Diocesan Arms, with supporting angels
17. Foster was possibly in hospital for an operation on his spine
18. Eric Gill died on the 17th of November 1940. The 'Great Crucifix' on the East Front of the Cathedral was carved after the war by Anthony Foster, following the original joint-design of Gill and the architect Edward Maufe

First published on the occasion of the service of thanksgiving for the life and work of David Kindersley at St James's Church, Piccadilly, London on 2 October 1995

Presented as a keepsake in November 1995 to the Wynkyn de Worde Society of which David Kindersley was a member from 1960 to 1995, Chairman 1976 and Honorary President from 1988 to 1995

Additional copies available from
David Kindersley's Workshop
152 Victoria Road
Cambridge CB4 3DZ
Price £5.00

ISBN 1 874426 04 X

Typeset by Tautos Ltd Cambridge in Octavian designed by
David Kindersley and Will Carter
Paper donated by MoDo Merchants
Illustrations scanned by Essex Colour Services, Southend, Essex
Covers printed by The Cloister Press, Cambridge
Printed and bound by BAS Printers Ltd, Over Wallop, Hampshire